David's Encyclopedia of
Useless Knowledge
(Poetry of Life)

David's Encyclopedia of Useless Knowledge
(Poetry of Life)

by

David E. Hungate

ISBN: 1-58820-247-X

1stBooks - rev. 9/20/00

Written For You

What do I know of setting words to verse?
Accept and enjoy them for better or worse.
These stories of trails, triumphs and love
Must be sent from somewhere above.

Somehow these words just come to me,
So I must write them and set them free.
Some of these poems are a little bit coarse
But I make no apologies and have no remorse.

There comes a time when we must speak out,
And face some facts on what life's about.
Sometimes they offer a different view,
Please enjoy them, they're written for you.

DEDICATION

A friend of mine, Rhonda McCalester, was the first person to suggest that I write this book, so if it contains anything that you do not like or that offends you….blame her.

Dave Hungate
April 1999

This book is dedicated to my wife, Jennifer

Thirty-four years of wedded bliss
On Life's roller coaster ride.
Thirty-four years of ups and downs
With you there by my side.

We cannot promise tomorrow
Life is a curious game.
But if I could, I would ask for more
Lots more of the same.

It's a wild ride, so hang on tight
As wing flows through your hair,
And know, yes know if nothing else
I do, yes I really do care.

Love ya
Dave

TABLE OF CONTENTS

Career Marine

Written for a career Marine, Stephen Bush,
By a Reserve Marine. Once a Marine, Always a Marine.

I turned 21 while serving in Korea.
Lying in a fox hole "bad idea".
A Sergeant friend who knew me well,
Said your just 21, already in Hell.

He gave me Jack Daniels in a cup.
Happy Birthday Marine, keep it up.
Deciding to make a Marine career,
I did my duty year after year.

Now I'm retired as a proud Marine,
Thinking of the things I've seen.
Not all bad and not all good,
Changing nothing if I could.

We each have only one life to live,
We each have only so much to give.
Retired Marine with piece of mind.
Tranquil peace that's hard to find.

Traveling the country with my wife.
Enjoying living the "Book of Life".

Dave Hungate
December 1999

Davita

My little nutty buddy who grew up long ago.
My little nutty buddy, a pleasure just to know.
In my treasure chest of life, this one is a pearl.
My little nutty buddy, Still Daddy's little girl.

She must live her own life and do what she must do.
Treasures such as this one, the world has very few.
I know that I must share her, that little girl of mine.
So others can enjoy her, at least part of the time.

Don't let the world abuse her, my precious little jewel.
If you're the one who wrongs her, get ready for a dual.
My little nutty buddy shares my blood and my name.
I let the world share her but she's mine just the same.

Love Ya Lots,
Dad

Indecision

Indecision is something that plagues us all.
We're not able or willing to make the call.
How many battles or wars have been lost?
What price have we paid in human cost?

Because someone, somewhere couldn't decide.
Indecision combined with ignorant pride.
There must be a meaning we're looking to find.
But were not quite able to make up our mind.

Dave Hungate
October 1999

Writers

Too many writers distort the facts.
Recording or reporting histories acts.
Most cowboys were not exciting enough
So the writers made them honest and tough.

Truth holds more interest than any lie.
Who knows the reason they continue to try?
We tend to believe everything in print.
As glitter of gold or money from the Mint.

So many of the stories we all believe
Only the wildest writer could conceive.
All writers and reporters are not crooks
So we must believe what's in their books.

Some of the writings are just so much rot,
But better than nothing and all we've got.
Histories mysteries confusing and grand,
Of many great people who made their stand.

Nostradomus and the apostle John
Predicted events of today and beyond.
If all these people heard stories we spin.
Some wouldn't recognize as talking of them.

Dave Hungate
October 1999

Thanksgiving

Thanksgiving should not be just one day.
Nor should that be the only time we pray.
Talk to your God at least once an hour,
Don't wait until your life turns sour.

Any little thing or a simple "thank you".
He will acknowledge anything you do.
Use fully that day in late November,
Enjoy your family and your God remember.

Cultivate, practice and nurture love.
Receiving guidance from the one above.
Have fun with this, don't make it a chore.
Soon you will hunger and thirst for more.

You'll be more convincing when you say.
Have a great, yes great Thanksgiving Day!

Dave Hungate
September 1999

13

Splintered Love

Love can be a many-splintered thing.
You fall in love, and you buy a ring.
Then get married to start a new life,
Facing the world as husband and wife.

You begin to learn what this is about.
As nerves get frayed you begin to shout.
Were not quite sure of what we did.
We better be right, we're having a kid.

Then life plays one more little trick.
You now have to work, even when sick.
The house is clean the beds are made,
We're out of money and bills aren't paid.

If you're lucky enough to a little acquire.
Something breaks or you'll have a flat tire.
We try not to let it get us down.
Were already working the clock around.

A truly good marriage is a work of art.
But it's easy, so easy to grow apart.
You must find someone, someone to blame.
You begin to wonder if you're going insane.

By now there's two kids and one on the way.
Lord gives the strength to handle the day.
Things aren't as bad as they sometimes seem,
Because over the years we became a team.

Dave Hungate
October 1999

Winners and Losers

Are there really any winners, true winners at war?
If we openly, objectively, the facts explore.
There are plenty of losers we can be sure.
Tragic atrocities both sides must endure.

We must stand up and do what is right.
Sometimes that leaves no choice but to fight.
Now the tough part, who's right and who's wrong.
Both have their reasons, the feeling is strong.

It isn't by chance nor is it just luck.
Somebody, somewhere is making a buck.
Politicians and business continue lying.
While our children are fighting and dying.

Patriotic Americans, loyal to the core.
Don't they deserve a whole lot more?
Let's try telling truth, telling all facts.
So they have conviction behind their acts.

We don't have all answers, we wish we did.
Don't think them stupid because they're a kid.
War fought by the young is as old as time.
Let's put politicians on the front line.

Keep them there so they stay in touch.
If nothing else, they wouldn't talk so much.

Dave Hungate
October 1999

Pony

My daughter had a pony that ran away,
On a cold and rainy September day.
I've got more temper than anyone needs
And I was chasing him in waist high weeds.

He managed to stay just beyond my reach.
He knew there was lesson I wanted to teach.
He finally stopped and did what I said.
By that time I was wishing him dead.

I was mad and wet and chilled to the bone.
I said, come on sucker, I'm riding home.
I jumped on his muddy, wet, slippery back.
If not for him, I'd still be in the sack.

He took off like we were running a race.
I slid around his neck and stared at his face.
I said whoa please whoa you son of a B.
I swear to this day that he was laughing at me.

At home I found a board about ten feet long.
I had blood in my eyes and was ready but wrong.
I tried hard to kill him as he jumped away.
He enjoyed every minute of our sadistic play.

I ended up exhausted and laying in the mud.
With about as much class as Elmer Fudd.
I lay there a while and laughed at myself.
Took the board in the barn and put on a shelf.

When I think of that pony and our rotten day,
I guess he taught me some things in a way.

Dave Hungate
September 1999

16

Green Rock

We met again in '99, that great old Green Rock bunch.
A super time was had by all, at least that is my hunch.
No dignitaries among us, just common, working folks.
With lots of crazy stories and some with rotten jokes.

We ourselves don't understand why this is so much fun.
Talking, laughing, joking of when our lives begun.
Think about minorities and those who are outcast.
In almost any contest we would have placed "dead last ".

We've met lots of people and some of them were great.
The Green Rock gang included a pleasure caused by fate.
I search my mind; I try to think of other groups like this.
I know lots of other people and some I dearly miss.

But something about that old Green Rock Tribe,
It seems pale written words can not describe.
Our lives are so much different but still a common bond.
That rowdy, rascals, goofy gang that we have grown so fond.

Compared to our last weekend, the world is calm and still.
Cherish memories till we meet again, as I'm sure we will.

Dave Hungate
May 1999

Audrey

I know a gal named Audrey, she's an angel in disguise.
Always helping someone, even those she could despise.
Always in the background, she desires no applause.
But ready to support and help with any worthy cause.

Her eyes kind and gentle like beacons from her heart.
You know without a question, she will always do her part.
She's a common lovely lady with normal human frails.
This lovely, lovely, lady who's blazing human trails.

I think she is infected with the need to really care.
She seems to be contagious as she teaches us to share.
This sweetheart of a lady, this angel in disguise.
When rating friends to all, deserves the greatest prize.

Dave Hungate
May 1999

The Family Farm

I love family farmers and the farm.
Please let this poem do them no harm.
How much longer can these farmers last?
Are we facing facts or living in the past.

So many others have come and gone.
How did the farmers hang on this long?
Butcher shops, hardware and grocery store
Gas stations, restaurants and many more.

Generations worked hard with family pride.
When the end came we took it in stride.
The government programs have been a joke.
Bureaucrats argue while farmers go broke.

Restrictions, subsidies, and good intentions,
Along with so many disaster preventions.
Drought's, floods and storms to name few.
Nothing seems to work, whatever we do.

Are we innocent victims of unfair trade?
Or simply not able to make the grade?
Questions come easy, answers come hard,
Like a gambler who's playing his last card.

Lord if you're listening let me be wrong.
Please let family farmers come back strong.

Dave Hungate
September, 1999

Compared to What?

When we think of what we have or have not.
I guess many times, it's compared to what.
A beggar for a sandwich gives thanks galore.
While people with millions still want more.

Are we to dumb to know when enough is enough?
As old prizefighters thinking we're tough.
Why can't we enjoy what we have instead?
Grasping for more until we are dead.

You can't take it with you or so I'm told,
So enjoy it now before you're too old.
I can see it now in your obituary.
He is the richest man in the Cemetery.

Dave Hungate
October 1999

Baggage or Garbage

Only with strangers do you carry no baggage.
What many people see is so much garbage.
Whether you're good or bad, rich or poor.
People think they know what you stand for.

Right or wrong, you are judged today,
By the way you reacted yesterday.
Are you living life or maybe just living?
A life that takes without much giving.

You've made many mistakes as we all do,
Dig a little deeper and find the real you.
Add a little adventure and take some chances,
Pay no attention to slurs and glances.

Take a little trip; hit the road my friend,
Destination decided when you get to the end.
No place to start, no place to finish,
As your mind and soul and body replenish.

Make a clean break with nothing to regret.
Then turn yourself loose, forgive and forget.
Security is nothing but a frame of mind.
Who knows, who knows, what you may find.

As you travel these roads near and far.
Try to see people for what they are.
Different from you, but still not wrong.
What do you care, you won't be there long.

If you come back to complete an objective,
You'll be living life with new perspective.
Don't live a life you hate or dread.
Living like that is like living dead.

Dave Hungate
October 1999

21

Ideas

To many ideas go down as cheap talk.
Like a child who fails to learn to walk.
These amazing ideas of yours and mine.
Why do we waste the effort and time?

We fail to develop or perfect anything.
As a beautiful voice that will never sing.
Amazing ideas that are never perfected.
Are we that afraid of being rejected?

Most great people thought of as kooks.
Guided by goblins, witches or spooks.
Were just common people who had the guts,
Not to care whom thought they were nuts.

To tell the truth, you're strange anyhow.
So please do something, please do it now.

Dave Hungate
October 1999

Kissing

Kissing spreads germs, I've heard stated.
So kiss me quick, I'm vaccinated.
Pucker up baby and put it on me.
I'm about as ready as I can be.

My lips are hot and my face is warm.
My love for you is a raging storm.
Searching for you all my life it seems,
The answers to any man's perfect dreams.

If you don't like it, I'll give it back.
Along with a hug to take up the slack.
Please, oh please don't let me miss.
The chances of lifetime's perfect kiss.

Dave Hungate
October 1999

Woulda, Coulda, Shoulda

I didn't but I shoulda
I wouldn't but I coulda
I wanta and I mighta
I haven't but I'm gunna

Or I'm not a gunna maybe
I canna if I wanta.
Maybe I should waita.
And see if then I canna.

By then I may not wanta.
I'm afraid if I don't goa.
I'll always think I shoulda.
And maybe wish I hadda.

Dave Hungate
October 1999

Nurses

Why would anyone want to be a nurse?
Forced to take us for better or worse.
Everyone they meet is somehow needing,
Impaired or sick or sometimes bleeding.

They listen to us, we complain and groan,
Not allowed any problems of their own.
Doctors seem to carry a certain prestige,
Not allowed the nurse who is under siege.

The Nurses end up with the dirty work.
Remaining professional, poised and pert.
Feeling bad, our patience wears thin.
Not for a moment, do we consider them.

Reflect a little to consider these verses.
Thank God and them, for wonderful nurses.

Dave Hungate
October 1999

Please, Hurry Up!

My Lord travels with me every place I go,
But sometimes he seems to be awfully slow.
I know that someday he will fill my cup,
But is there some way to hurry things up?

Dear Lord understand, no offense is intended.
It's hard to be patient when over extended.
Streets lined with gold are so often stated.
Right now I would settle for some gold plated.

In heaven we'll have such a vast amount.
Is there a way to draw from that account?
In heaven we know a new day will dawn.
Don't let me be lacking or over drawn.

With your infinite wisdom I thought somehow
You might know a way to give me some now.
So many prayers I know you must get,
This has to be weirdest one yet.

I'll try to be happy with whatever you do.
Please keep in mind, I'm counting on you.

Dave Hungate
October 1999

Baboons

I don't believe the theory of evolution,
But that may well be the only solution.
To explain people, I've met in saloons
Who I'm sure, are related to baboons.

Smelling something like an old sweat sock.
Their intelligence rivals an average rock.
They have an opinion on everything
From politics to what people sing.

They voice their opinions loud and strong.
You can almost bet, they'll be wrong.
If evolution's theory is so great.
Why do they remain in the primate state?

Dave Hungate
October 1999

Addiction

What you will do next is beyond prediction,
Because of your alcohol and drug addiction,
You're the one who started your wanton abuse.
Now you're trying to use it as a feeble excuse.

You get another chance and again you fail.
Are we wasting time, do you belong in jail?
You're fooling no one by the things you say,
Lock them up, and throw the key away.

I never met anyone who jail helped much.
Just one more thing to serve as a crutch.
Chain gang time will get your attention,
And help you understand drug prevention.

A few years of this to learn production;
Plus a few more years working construction.
Don't even think about getting paid.
You're paying for mistakes you made.

By now drugs and alcohol are forgotten,
Unless your memory is terribly rotten.
If you get out and once again you forget,
We'll bring you back and remind you a bit.

I search mind and soul to find compassion.
To treat you at least in a civil fashion.
Don't blame us for the things we must do.
How you are treated depends on you.

Dave Hungate
October 1999

Automobile

Nothing on earth can make us feel
Like compassion for an automobile.
A 40 Ford, an Edsel or a model A,
Or a mid to late 50's Chevrolet.

How good they are doesn't matter much,
As long as they had that special touch.
A Lincoln Zephyr has never been mine.
They had the worlds, greatest design.

Resembling a bullet for a powerful gun,
Poised like a sprinter ready to run.
Silent prestige of going first class.
Standing still, they looked fast.

They create more for each generation
From minds of men artistic creation.
A passion carried from cradle to grave.
It's funny what memory, chooses to save.

Dave Hungate
October 1999

Medical Assistant

I met a lady who was quite persistent.
I learned the meaning of medical assistant.
I'm still not certain I know for sure.
But please, oh please don't tell her.

It's a level between doctor and nurse.
Or did I get that somehow in reverse?
Is it the nurse's assistant or the Doc's,
Or the person in charge of giving shots?

How can we possibly give them their due?
When we can't understand what they do.
As I get in deeper, and more confused
I hope this lady is only amused.

How we say it doesn't matter that much.
Thank God for them, their personal touch.
Thank God they are smarter than you and I.
Who don't understand, however we try.

Dave Hungate
October 1999

Regis and Cathy Lee

I sat down to watch TV
But didn't want Regis and Cathy Lee.
I watch them often, they are good,
But wanted something else, if I could.

How could this giant industry panel,
Let them be on every channel?
Forty two stations did I turn,
My cool calm nature starting to burn.

You can watch weather, sports or news,
Would be politicians expressing views.
The only thing left for us to see,
Were dear old Regis and Cathy Lee.

I went to sleep; nothing left it seems,
But Regis and Cathy were in my dreams.
I went to a doctor, said help me quick,
This time I'm really, really sick.

I told about Regis and Cathy Lee,
He said the same thing happened to me.
Drink some water and take these pills,
They will cure most of your ills.

Now I'm sedated and watching TV.
Enjoying Regis and Cathy Lee.

Dave Hungate
March 1999

Memory

A show on television caught my attention.
It had new facts about memory retention.
It seems the age theory is much over sold.
Memory needn't be worse when one gets old.

With proper actions memory is retained,
And almost always abilities regained.
Exercise-- mental and physical most in need.
Memory improves more as more we read.

Intellectual stimulation, most any kind
Improves our memory, attitude and mind.
It sounds like a joke but the experts say
To improve your memory, eat an apple a day.

Anything retained for more than a minute.
Your memory forever will have that in it.
Everyone you meet repeat the name out loud.
Repeat to yourself until it is not a cloud.

It all boils down to the fact we get lazy.
Which makes our memory functions hazy.
Exercise, eat right and read a bit.
Keep your memory, mind and body fit.

Nothing is lost, if it doesn't improve.
Get out of the rut and into the groove.

Dave Hungate
October 1999

Vagabond

I'm a Vagabond on life's highway.
No where to go, no reason to stay.
I was raised by a wandering flock,
All my life I've been in hock.

I've been hurt so bad, I no longer feel
There's nothing left for time to heal.
Just a lonely bum, without a home,
In a strangers world where ever I roam.

My broken heart is too sad to cry.
Nobody cares if I live or die.
Why Oh Why was I ever born.
To live a life that is this forlorn.

I'm not too worried about life's end.
But I'd like to know, when will mine begin.
You like others, just pass me by.
WHY, OH WHY, OH WHY,OH WHY.

I guess I'll wonder till I die.
OH WHY, OH WHY, OH WHY, OH WHY.

Dave Hungate
March 1999

Cry, Cry, Cry

It seems there are people prone to cry.
They themselves don't understand why.
They cry when happy and cry of when sad,
They cry in good times and cry in bad.

It works like a built-in finger bowl,
For washing eye's and cleansing soul.
People who are not the type to whine;
When bawling is done, they'll be fine.

Jump right in, get the bawling done.
Shake it off and it's time for fun.
Never learning, with hearts on sleeve,
Sharing everyone's reason to grieve.

I guess in a way there's compensation.
They cry with joy at a celebration.
Passionate people with feelings deep,
A friend in need, a friend to keep.

With all this built up energy.
Not one you want as an enemy.
It seems to work so who cares why,
So get in there and cry, cry, cry.

Dave Hungate
October 1999

Corporations

Corporations have no souls; they have hearts of stone.
Build your life around them, and find yourself alone.
Many have nice slogans and speak of corporate pride,
They want you to smile as you take your final ride.

Most of them have merits that we must all admire.
Thank them for the standards they help us acquire.
Quality, health and safety raise standard of living.
Plus charities and benefits to which they are giving.

Corporations are fine and have their place,
Just don't get lost in the corporate race.
Hard work is virtue and it's good to have goals;
Remember this warning, corporations have no souls.

Dave Hungate
November 1999

Friends

Friends like you are a treasure for sure,
When facts are facts and thoughts are pure.
Give me a hug along with a smile.
Just stop by and visit a while.

Walk right in and sit yourself down.
Turn yourself loose, act like a clown.
Chat for a while, tell stories without end,
You're always welcome at my house my friend.

Dave Hungate
October 1999

Semper Fi

Some People wonder and question why,
Marines have a saying of Semper Fi.
Always faithful is what that means,
Always faithful, that's the Marines.

Willing to serve any place on Earth.
Ready always to prove their worth.
Most are hoping wars will cease
As they are keeping world peace.

They know too well, war isn't fun.
Always faithful till job is done.
Serving their country, serving well.
Sometimes facing horrors of hell.

Why would anyone be a Marine?
Naturally tough, brave or mean?
Just common people like you and I.
Who understand the words Semper Fi.

Next time you vote let out a cry,
"Thank God, and Marines......Semper Fi."

Dave Hungate
December 1999

New Day

As the tide goes out in the morning
And the beach is left behind
During the night a new beach was formed
The sand was left refined.

The sandpiper does his morning dance
And the sea gulls as thick as flies
They seem to be talking to each other
With their attending screeches and cries.

A crane stands alone for awhile
And surveys everything on the beach.
While fisherman who are catching nothing
Need to learn what he could teach.

The sun has a show of its' own
I swear for awhile it was yawning
As the clouds move out of his way
Once again a new day is dawning.

The sea is a silver blue blanket
As it moves away from the shore
We know it'll be back tonight
To bring us a whole lot more.

Dave Hungate
March 2000

Green River Methodist

Green River ,Illinois was the start of our searches.
Looking for classic, unique or unusual Churches.
This was such a great place to start our search.
In front of our own "House on the Prairie Church".

Standing on a hill with so many years of pride.
With a welcome to all, the doors open wide.
People from everywhere stop to take pictures.
They care very little about size or fixtures.

Most are relating to somewhere in their mind.
Where life held peace and people were kind.
Their childhood memories cause them to search.
For a place like this "House on the Prairie Church.

Dave Hungate
April 2000

America the Beautiful

America the beautiful is more than what we say;
America the beautiful in almost every way.
If we were given options where to have a birth.
We would choose America over any place on earth.

We know there are problems to which we must attend.
Plus many lofty goals to which we must ascend.
Give thanks to God for those who've gone before.
For gifts we have today and dreams of so much more.

Use wisely all resources and replenish as we go,
So future generations will also learn to know.
America the beautiful that lives within our heart;
To live and grow more beautiful, we must do our part.

Dave Hungate
October 1999

Sleep Damage

I was feeling fine when I went to bed.
Now there are Jack Hammers in my head.
My hair is a mess, my eyes bloodshot.
My body is cold and my face is hot.

Even my skin and hair seem to hurt.
My eyeballs itch as full of dirt.
My mind is fried; my life is paused,
Look at the problem sleep has caused.

We partied for hours feeling fine.
Now there are jellyfish in my spine.
I was King Farouk and Ali Kahn.
The smartest and toughest all in one.

Now it seems awfully hard to find,
Anything makes sense in my mind.
Last night I was smart and terribly tough.
This morning I'm feeling mighty rough.

I'm feeling better and managed to smile.
I'll be strong enough to stand after while.
I'll kickstart my mind and make it think,
As soon as I find a powerful drink.

A promise to myself, I must keep.
I must remember never to sleep.
I'll party again and have such fun.
Forgetting the damage sleep has done.

Dave Hungate
October 1999

Spiders' Harvest

Look closely at a spider's web,
With many victims hanging dead.
It's a simple and ingenious plan.
That may be adapted someday by man.

It catches, dries and stores food.
Waiting for him in a festive mood.
If patience is virtue, he's on top,
Serenely awaiting a bountiful crop.

He builds a Web with little effort,
Sets and waits for financial reports.
A prosperous year or lean instead.
Does he know he'll soon be dead?

All he saved will soon be gone.
Eating nothing, waiting to long.

Dave Hungate
October 1999

Freedom of Mind

Look up, look up, look up to the sky.
Let your mind wonder and question why.
Look for answers or at least a clue,
With nothing between divinity and you.

Ralph Waldo Emerson made that quote.
And coined phrases of positive note.
Our mind has power for limitless gains,
Unless we ourselves keep it in chains.

Common sense or caution has its place.
But should not keep you out of the race.
We blindly accept whatever we're told.
We don't get smarter we just get old.

Dream a little let thought run wild.
Imagine or fantasize, as would a child.
You'll be surprised, and much enjoy,
Letting yourself be a little boy.

Understanding puzzles without fears.
Having fun and erasing the years.
Feeling and being smarter by far.
Than anyone else thinks you are.

Dave Hungate
October 1999

Quad Cities

We've traveled the cities from Phoenix to Nome,
But nothings as great as coming back home.
When they ask "Where Ya From?" we're proud to say.
Were from the "Quad Cities" USA

Tri-Cities, Quad Cities, Quint Cities and more,
Great little towns on the Mississippi Shore.
That's where the river runs east and west.
That's one more reason Quad Cities is best.

You can fish or play with anything that floats,
Or sit on the banks and watch riverboats.
We've got bike paths, benches, and parks of all kinds,
Nothing can stop us when we make up our minds.

We are known worldwide for machinery we build,
But that says nothing of our literary Guild.
We have colleges, museums, and very great schools,
Just hometown folks, but nobody fools.

Come and see us sometime, we'll be your host.
You'll understand why we love home the most.
Nice to see you again, but again we must say.
Were heading back home "Quad cities" USA.

Dave Hungate
June 1999

Johnny Joe

I know a guy who is named Johnny Joe.
He can be a pain but a pleasure to know.
He's getting old but still moving on.
I nicknamed him Ole There and Gone.

Illinois to Minnesota he went on a trip.
Couldn't find an address so lost his grip.
He turned around and came back home.
His would-be greeters were standing alone.

The devil himself couldn't catch Johnny Joe.
When his life is over and it's his time to go.
We may ask which way did Johnny Joe move on?
The devil will say, he's been here and gone.

Dave Hungate
May 1999

Strangers Smiles

I see a stranger once in a while.
They have a gorgeous sincere smile.
Don't know them or know of their name,
That's even better, wouldn't be the same.

On life's highway of rough rugged miles,
It's nice to see a stranger that smiles.

Dave Hungate
May 1999

Anna, Sweet Anna

Anna, sweet Anna was stubborn as a mule,
Weathered by life and nobody's fool.
She weighed 90 pounds soaking wet,
Straight forward as a person can get.

She was quite a lady in her day,
She had a kick shift in her model A.
Body so slight but her heart was large,
There was no question who was in charge.

I loved the stories she used to spin,
For the moment she was young again.
I could hear the same story numerous times,
She kept your interest by changing lines.

There was no ill will in her exaggeration,
It just added spice to the situation.
There are not many people on earth like her,
But many of us wish there were.

Dave Hungate
February 1999

Alike But Different

Happy is a person who has found their niche,
No longer concerned with being in a clique.
Ready to attempt anything they aspire,
Fulfilling their dreams and wildest desire.

It may be a place for them to call home.
It may be good health or freedom to roam.
Your wildest desire may not interest me,
Alike but different, that's supposed to be.

You love to hunt and you love to fish,
That's great for you but not my wish.
Some hate to travel or fly in a plane,
They think those who do must be insane.

Others think its torture to travel by car,
If they go anywhere, it's not very far.
Go camping or travel cross-country by bike.
Enjoy and be thankful we're not all alike.

Dave Hungate
February 2000

Seventy Plus

I like talking to people who are 70 plus.
They know the meaning of "in God we trust".
They grew up during the great depression.
They experienced first-hand segregation.

Then World War II broke families apart.
Memories vivid in their mind and heart.
Men had to leave children and wives
And all too many gave their lives.

Some men who returned refused to talk.
Other men returned unable to walk.
They like women with husbands imparted,
Were near middle age when life started.

Many carry scars that may not show.
We can learn a lot from things they know.
Most are ignored because they are old.
They are a treasure more precious than gold.

Dave Hungate
December 1999

Housekeeper

We marry young and we set our course.
A few years later it ends in divorce.
She's a real housekeeper like they said,
Got rid of me, kept the house instead.

Sounds like an awful strong penalty,
For having just one little infidelity.
Now I'm out looking for women again
In all the taverns and houses of sin.

If a dog could carry a coffee cup
Instead of a wife, I'd look for a pup.
If I could find the one I would choose,
It would also be able to carry my shoes.

I would train it the way I want it to be.
I would know for certain that it loved only me.
Now I'm setting at home with lonely nights.
Understanding the meaning of women's rights.

Dave Hungate
December 1999

Foxhole

Everyone prays from an old foxhole,
With a heavy heart and a wounded soul.
If you help us now, we'll never forget.
I wonder if God says yeah, I'll bet.

In good times, we're proud of ourselves,
While dusty old Bibles' sit on shelves.
Are we ignorant fools, weak of mind?
Continually looking for peace of mind.

Very few, a lesson will actually learn.
When their life takes a sudden upturn.
Most will forget to remember their fate,
And suddenly think themselves as great.

We shouldn't blame God all that much.
When we again failed to keep in touch.
Every so often we need to console.
Remembering well a lonely foxhole.

Dave Hungate
October 1999

Too Little Too Late

Some people complain about everything,
Even how long the church bells ring?
One has pleasure from bells that chime,
The next hears noise invading his time.

It's not their desire to be rude,
It's just a result of their attitude.
One person enjoys life-giving rain,
To others it is a gloom-ridden pain.

Is it always too cold or too hot?
Can't we enjoy things we have got?
Enjoy, enjoy, because life is great
Or you may have too little too late.

Dave Hungate
January 2000

Shopping

I lost my wife while at WalMart.
Shopping must be a woman's art.
Waiting for hours at the checkout line,
Everyone else was doing just fine.

I finally broke down and bought a bike.
After walking miles on a fruitless hike.
I rode that bike for so many miles,
Up and down the endless aisles.

It was good to feel her gentle touch.
She really hadn't aged that much.
Never again will I venture that far.
Go ahead dear, I'll wait in the car.

Dave Hungate
January 2000

Porcelain Throne

The only place in the world you are truly alone
Is when you're setting on a porcelain throne.
It's built as a place for people to stink,
But it works just fine if you sit and think.

Don't sit too long or you'll look real dumb,
With a ring on your rear and legs are numb.
When you walk you waddle like Donald Duck.
It's a full-time job just standing up.

The next time you want it to be all alone,
Be King for a while on your porcelain throne.

Dave Hungate
December 1999

Twelve Great Months

January comes to start a New Year.
Like a newborn child, without fear.
Full of promise, faith and trust,
Enjoy January that's a must.

February has a wintry flair,
Good and bad for us to share.
Pity the person who doesn't know
The cleansing effect of falling snow.

March, great March comes marching in,
Sweeping the world with its wind.
Blowing winter out so it can bring
A glorious time we call Spring.

April showers fall to nourish earth,
Giving life to all, a total rebirth.
Sprouting flowers and towering trees
Plus so much more that nobody sees.

May is known for its beautiful flowers
Painting the world with mystic powers.
It's hard to find a more perfect day
Than many we've received in May.

A favorite of most is the month of June
With warm calm days and a lover's moon.
Enjoy the nights and enjoy the days
Time passes on but the memory stays.

July is the time for summertime fun.
Boating or swimming or bask in the sun.
Still more fun is within your reach,
If you party all night on a sandy beach,.

August arrives with a lot of heat
And long summer nights hard to beat.
It's hot and muggy without much air,
Pretend you're on an island anywhere.

Colors of autumn we will long remember
They start to appear in late September.
Any artist alive would give his heart
To master the beauty of natures art.

October tells us that fall is here.
Enjoy each day because winter is near.
It's picnic time and time to cookout.
Times like this are what life's about.

November is here, time for Thanksgiving.
Thank the Lord for the pleasure of living.
Families everywhere should get together
To love each other, forget the weather.

December comes and a year has passed
Reminding us that life goes fast.
Charge on ahead with nothing to fear
Thank the Lord for another great year.

Dave Hungate
February 2000

Hero or Traitor

If something happened to force our hand,
Would we be willing to take a stand?
Fighting for a cause, would we be strong?
Are we smart enough to know what's wrong?

Revolution that created the United States
Produced for us the greatest of greats.
They are heroes to us with very good reason,
To the British, traitors guilty of treason.

In Germany when Hitler came to rule.
Would we have been his ignorant fools?
Some thought him great and sent to save;
Some believed this all the way to the grave.

If the same thing happened in the world today,
Would we know what to do or to say?
Would we know how to make the right choice?
Would we be willing to cast our voice?

Very few called are heroes from any war.
Lived to enjoy what they fought for.
Questions without answers for us all.
Would we be willing to accept the call?

Dave Hungate
February 2000

Women

When women go to battle, the world should give in.
You know before the start that she is going to win.
Like David and Goliath fighting with slings,
Who knows the extra powers a woman brings?

Many men with strength that is beyond belief
Are asking a woman somewhere for relief.
With a voice sometimes that can hardly be heard,
She brings down the toughest without a word.

Every person who has ever set a foot on earth,
Owes a woman somewhere for giving them birth.
So world please listen, you don't have a chance,
She can kill some people with just a glance.

Don't even think about starting a fight.
You are playing my friend with dynamite.

Dave Hungate
April 2000

Shells

Gathering shells on a sandy beach
Mother Nature has a lot to teach.
So little of life is really known
Each of these shells had a life of their own.

Even the waves as they dip and dive
You'd swear that sometimes they must be alive.
Not only the tides ebb and flow
When there gone where did they go.

As the waves get higher there is still more
As the water itself starts to talk and roar.
Are all these waves like a sister and brother?
That sometimes has to holler at each other?

The waves move the beaches as they sing and dance
And this doesn't happen just by chance.
And once again Mother Nature teaches
Keep it clean and wash your beaches.

Dave Hungate
March 2000

Self Imposed

Most problems in life are self- imposed
Not fickle fate as many has proposed.
We eat, drink, smoke and talk too much,
Then make excuses to serve as a crutch.

We lie, cheat and steal from each other,
Often as close as a spouse or a brother.
We hurt each other without good reason,
Sometimes committing family treason.

We are not talking of people who are bad
I guess that is why the story is so sad.
This is a person who really tries,
He is one of the good guys.

Dave Hungate
April 2000

No Intelligent Life

One day some Martians came to earth
To check it out for what it's worth.
First they saw a longhaired hippie
And a scientist who was rather dippy.

Next there was a motorcycle gang
Who greeted them with profane slang.
Then some golfers trying to score
And yelling something about four.

They reported back, nothing to fear.
There's no intelligent life around here.

Dave Hungate
March 2000

My Southern Bell

Carolyn , sweet Carolyn, that spicy southern bell
I love to sit and listen to the stories she can tell.
She sings like an angel, she loves to sing and play.
When she gets her dander up don't get in her way.

She is a friend to all who need a friend
Her persistence seems to know no end.
Carolyn, sweet Carolyn, that spicy southern bell
Sweet, kind and gentle with a temper straight from
HA HA HA

Her faith in God deep seeded, demeanor sweet and kind,
Once she makes her decisions you won't change her mind.
She opens up her heart and opens up her home,
Much like an oasis from the highways that you roam.

Dave Hungate
March 2000

Just a Human Being

Nothing wrong with people having pride
But all too often there is a darker side.
We put some people on a pedestal
As to enshrine them in fine crystal.

Politician, movie star, parent or child
Can become confused or even wild.
They, like we, are so often tempted
And few if any are ever exempted.

Entitled to frailties, mistakes or sin.
Where did all our misgivings begin?
Maybe it started with the kings of old.
Considered as smart, courageous or bold.

Some were revered long after dead
Ignorant, pompous and often inbred,
We know in our hearts without seeing.
After all they are just a human being.

Dave Hungate
March 2000

Getting Fired

There is nothing wrong with getting fired.
It can be a blessing to the truly inspired.
I've been in position to fire a few
And been fired myself a time or two.

When they are released without strings
They go on to bigger and better things.
People with degrees from schools so fine
Spend their lives on an assembly line.

With families to feed they dare not coast
And sell their lives to who pays the most.
They keep trying but there's never enough
To get released from the golden handcuff.

Often true vocation comes after retired
So it's can be a blessing to just get fired.

Dave Hungate
March 2000

Clean Money

Remember if you don't want to look funny
Don't go swimming with a pocket full of money.
The bills come out and begin to float
They each look like a little green boat.

Fives and tens and twenties too
You hate to admit that they belong to you.
Dried out wrinkles don't go where they should
George and Abe never looked so good.

No longer greenbacks as they begin to turn yellow,
So you pass them along to some other fellow.
When you go swimming check your pocket
Or you'll end up with Abe looking like Davy Crockett.

It's bad enough when it is only you,
But everyone else will be laughing too.
In the background you'll here someone say
That guy has money to throw away.

He must not be all that mean
Because he washes his money to keep it clean.
Everybody has a laugh so it's okay
But I still must believe there's a better way.

Dave Hungate
March 2000

Ability Without Ambition

Ability without ambition is like a car with no motor,
Or flying in a helicopter without controls or a rotor.
Many times it is not because people want to shirk,
But somehow their guidance system doesn't work.

Some of them work for years and work very hard,
Then gamble everything on the turn of a card.
Many people who end up with too little too late
Like to blame someone else or at least on fate.

Their problems were caused by another's deed,
Never by their own foolish ignorance and greed.
Too many times this can be all too true,
But much more is decided by what you do.

Remember to enjoy life, not just survive
You'll never get out of this world alive.

Dave Hungate
March 2000

Palm Trees

Palm trees seem to grow best standing single file,
Straight, erect and tall - Military style.
In the south there are plenty, gracing every yard
Like Military sentries, always standing guard.

Many storms attack, but they stand and fight.
Erect as any soldier fighting through the night.
Just as any soldier, they know some must fall.
Just as any soldier, they still meet the call.

They seem to know the sun will soon arrive
Giving its blessings to the ones who survive.
They know time for passing will come another day,
And just like an old soldier, they'll just fade away.

Dave Hungate
April 2000

Dreamer

Behind every project there must be a dreamer
Forced sometimes to become a schemer.
Projects that are work, pleasure or fun
Someone must make sure the work gets done.

Not just a dreamer but a dreamer with vision,
Who tries hard to complete their mission.
A dreamer who is willing to work out a plan;
We all can do more than we think we can.

They look at the world from a different slant.
They don't acknowledge the word of can't.
Let yourself go and dream, dream, dream.
Things are not always the way they seem.

Dave Hungate
April 2000

Can We See God?

Can we see God through the darkness of today?
Do we have enough faith to show us the way?
Do we sometimes want to take the easy road?
Do we fail somehow to carry our load?

Do we tend to confuse ambition and greed?
There is a lot of difference in wants and need.
Do we take our lead from all the rest,
While telling God what we think is best?

If we keep trying to get everything right.
We will see God through the darkness of night.

Dave Hungate
April 2000

Saint Marks Whole Truth Church, Brinkley, Arkansas

Where two or more are gathered to praise his holy name;
Condition doesn't matter, to him they're all the same.
They may not take collection in any vast amounts.
That also doesn't matter, it's what's inside that counts.

It was twenty miles south of Brinkley, Arkansas
Beside an old , old country road, far from any law.
We saw a country Church that stood out so grand.
You could tell by looking, it was built by hand.

The shingles and the roofing missed a match by far.
Most of it was covered by paper made of tar.
This tiny little Church with shingles that are torn.
Extends a hearty welcome to all that are forlorn.

Dave Hungate
April 2000

My Life

I grew up poor, as poor as can be,
Couldn't afford the things that were free.
I lost my arm at age twenty-two
Doing the things that young guys do.
Me and a friend out having a blast,
Drinkin' a little and driving too fast.
We were just kids, so what the heck,
We hit a bridge, had one hell of a wreck.

The steering wheel pinned the driver in
So he was bruised but never broke skin.
It was 1 a.m. on a September day
And my arm was laying 30 foot away.
This sounds bad but it could have been worse,
Because under the bridge was a doctor and nurse.
They were just fishing is what they said,
If not for them, I would have been dead.

Somehow my arm got knocked over the side,
As I took that ambulance ride.
They found it two weeks later a few miles down river.
Thinking about it still makes me quiver.
I went into business with a brother of mine,
He was real smart so we did just fine.
Then I met a girl who became my wife,
And children came to bless our life.

They took me for better or worse
I think that for them it was more of a curse.
A few years' later things turned real sour
And most of the problems were out of our power.
The car business and the economy bust,
We kept riding hard , but choked by the dust.
I couldn't give up or go out on a whim
That was the least I owed them.

I was too dumb to quit ,too honest to rob,
So I had to go out and find a good job.
Time has passed and the children grown,
Fine young people out on their own.
All that's left is just mom and me,
For the first time in our lives we're really free.
I'm retired and Mom will soon
So if we want we can shoot for the moon.
All in all it's been a good life
And I owe most of that to a real good wife.

Dave Hungate
February 1999

My Family

You ask about my family,
And what it means to me.
Each person somewhat different,
As limbs are on a tree.

We all must go our separate ways,
And be what we must be.
But get our strength from the same roots,
As limbs do on a tree.

When storms come down upon us,
We bend but must not break.
We all must hold on tightly
For each other's sake.

Then soon the storm is over
And we all have lots of fun.
As we wave and swing so happily
As a tree does in the sun.

You see we're still a family
In good times and in bad,
And I'll remember always
The good times that we had.

So when it comes my turn to start
A family of my own,
I know we'll have some strong roots,
The seed already sown.

Davita Hungate
1982

My Daddy's Son

When I was a little boy and stood about three feet tall,
My Daddy picked me up and sat me on a four-foot wall.
Daddy was a lively man, always full of fun,
Then he reached out and said jump to me son.

Finally I got brave enough to jump off the wall,
Daddy just stepped back and watched me fall.
Daddy was a lively man, always full of fun,
That was Daddy's way of sayin', don't trust anyone.

You think that Daddy was too rough, well I guess in a way
But I remember what he taught, to this very day.
Daddy's lessons made me tough, made me strong and brave
That is why I'm standin' tall, peeing on his grave.

Daddy was a lively man, always full of fun,
Now my Daddy knows too well, that I am just his son.

Dave Hungate
February 1999

Politics

Who is the next we must impeach,
And what lesson must we teach?
I'd like to use this brain of mine
But I must vote the party line.

I can be tough, you bet I can
If the guy on trial was Republican.
Ole Billy Boy can't be a rat
He's a good and loyal Democrat!

He's made mistakes like we all do
Is that so different from me and you?
Poetic justice might be in store
If we ended up with President Gore.

We should let Billy off the hook,
But keep the records in the book.
And if a Republican happens to win
We'll start this nonsense all again!

We'll get him and get him good
And do the things we know we should
To rid the world of Republican scum,
And we'll show no mercy to that bum.

Who do the voters think they are
To listen to people like Kenneth Starr?
Just leave everything up to me
Hang Republicans, let Democrat go free!

Dave Hungate
March 1999

Grandkids

My granddaughter gave me a butterfly
Only she knows the reason why.
Who knows the mysteries that go untold
In the mind of any five-year old?

There's one thing we both know for sure
It's not because I'm easy on her.
She's a pistol, a real fireball,
But I'm bull headed and I make the call.

And I guess that I will never know
Why that cheap little butterfly moved me so.
I carry it with me every day,
It's like having her along in a way.

Why would a silly little child's gift
Give a tough guy like me a lift?
I think it's because of unbridled love
Like that we receive from Him above.

We think we grow up
And I know this is wild,
But I guess in our hearts
We're all like a child.

Dave Hungate
March 1999

Marriage

When you marry and have children with wife,
The judge of judges said give him life.
So in your mind might as well console,
You are doing life without parole.

Before your children are totally grown,
Grandchildren come from the seeds you've sown.
On and on and on this goes,
As your bodily function slows.

I'm happy with this , so I have conceded
Enjoy the family, it's good to be needed.

Dave Hungate
March 1999

Our Little Girl

Jenny, Jenny, Jenny, Jenny
Our darling little girl.
Why must you grab a hold of life
And give it such a whirl.

You must think we're such a grouch
We're always raising hell.
But we hope that someday you will hear,
The stories that we tell.

About our little Jenny
And the great things she has done.
She's bright and smart and witty
And always full of fun.

When things are tough, we do our best
To guide you on life's way.
Never sure of what we do
Nor sure of what we say.

We want you to see the things
That we could never see.
We want you to be the person
We could never be.

We know with music, books, and life
It sometimes causes strain.
But at fourteen you've climbed to heights
That we could not attain.

But nothing means as much to us
No status we might have had
Could mean as much as to hear you say
"Hey kids, that's mom and dad.

Happy Birthday pal, and remember,
When we're making such a fuss
It really wouldn't matter much
If you didn't mean so much to us.

Dave Hungate
March 1999

People

I used to fear people from other places,
And dislike or mistrust other races.
Japanese, Chinese, Arab and Jew,
Their skin was different and their faces too.

Then I was foiled by the father of fate,
And had to live with those I could hate.
It wasn't by choice but it was a must,
And somehow found there were some I could trust.

How could this happen, how could this be
I found some of these people were better than me.
They were smarter and deeper but gentle and kind,
Actions like this will mess with your mind.

We are taught and told to look within
And not to judge by features or skin.
But nothing can teach like knowing them
With hearts much like an uncut gem.

To find people worth our trust
We must look beneath the crust.

Dave Hungate
March 1999

One Lifetime

I don't want you for forever
I just want you for awhile.
I don't want to make you sad,
I just want to make you smile.

I don't want to cause you trouble,
I don't want to be confused.
I want to have a good time,
I just want to be amused.

We can only live one lifetime,
It'll be over all too soon.
If you'll help me watch the sunset
Then I'll help you find the moon.

Dave Hungate
March 1999

Hooty Tooty Christian

You're a hooty tooty Christian, Caucasian, and Protestant.
Your thoughts are cast in concrete, never to be bent.
I hate to entertain these thoughts and be so awful rude,
But I'm getting sick and tired of your perfect attitude.

I know that you're good people and try to do so well,
But think I'd be more welcome in the fiery pits of hell.
I don't believe in Purgatory, but really wish I did,
It would be the perfect place for us who have backslid.

A place for normal people, just pretty decent folks,
Who try to do what's right, but still like dirty jokes.
You think I want to eat my cake, but want to have it too.
I guess I'll be rude again because it's not up to you.

You're a hooty, tooty, Christian, a person I admire,
But I don't think I'll be changing, I just have no desire.
I'm trying to speak frankly and trying to make you see
My fate is not your problem, it's between God and me.

Many people want your help, go listen to them moan.
Please go help the other guy, and please leave me alone.

Dave Hungate
May 1999

I Don't Care

I don't care, I don't care, I'm as free as the air.
Not a care in the air and I really don't care.
I'm retired at last, having a blast, I don't care.
The bills are all paid and the children are raised.

I'm as free as the air, not a care, not a care.
Like a bird on the wing, I wish I could sing.
I don't care, I don't care, I don't care.
I'm fat and I'm old but not hungry or cold.

I don't care, I don't care, I don't care.

Dave Hungate
May 1999

Mighty Oak

How could anyone be in love with a tree.
But that mighty oak meant a lot to me.
A violent storm brought its tragic end.
We mourn its death as loss of a friend.

Not like a human, that would be wrong.
More like a feeling you get from a song.
Some things soothe and warm your heart.
It was one of nature's works of art.

Our kids played there when very small.
For many years it was shade for us all.
A tree like this is so hard to find.
It will live forever in our mind.

Dave Hungate
May 1999

Misunderstood

Maybe I will write no more, but then again I might.
I seem to be misunderstood on much of what I write
I've heard of many artists, who draw for their own fun,
They work at it for hours and burn it when it's done.

As long as I am living to hear someone complain
I have a chance to talk to them, and hopefully explain.
My major information source is my pointed little head,
But what if I'm misunderstood long after I am dead.

Maybe I should bite my tongue, write only of what's good,
But I'm not one to shut my mouth even when I should.
Only I can set my course and decide which path to take,
I'd rather quit completely than become a wimpy fake.

It seems my writing has caused pain, the opposite intended.
Some of these are facts of life, some are just pretended.
My family means much more to me than any words on paper.
I think that I at least for now should find another caper.

I apologize to everyone for any pain I've caused.
I may not quit completely but at least for now I've paused.

Dave Hungate
May 1999

Sunday Best

I'm all dressed up in my Sunday best
But man I'm feeling' low.
I'm a boss down at the factory, so I guess I better go.
I know it would shock'em if I'm the one not to show.

We work so hard to be the best
To get ahead in these worldly games.
We wear these clothes to hide imperfections
While we reach for the wealth and fame.

When my life is over and it's time for me to go,
I'll be dressed in my Sunday best;
And when I arrive at the Pearly gates
I am plannin' on that eternal rest

But I'll hear Saint Peter
As he stops me to say,
"You can't come up here friend,
You're headin' the other way."

You sometimes tried real hard at life
But never quite made your goals
You're headed straight to Hades
You're in charge of shoveling coal.

So I guess I'll spend forever
Never quite makin' my goal
I'll be all dressed up in my Sunday best
And be in charge of shoveling coal.

Dave Hungate
March 1999

Poor Old Dad

When I was only ten years old
My dad was quite a man.
He was the smartest guy in town,
Perhaps in all the land.

Then only five years later
Poor old Dad just lost his mind
Someone who knew less than him
Was really hard to find.

His clothes were out of style
And his car was showing wear
He seemed to have no class or clout,
And didn't even care.

Now I'm almost twenty
I think Dad's coming around
Not solid as he once was, but back on solid ground.
If I work with him and guide him on the way
I'll get him back to his old self someday.

Mom and others say Dad has always been the same
But I know better so I'll play their little game.
Dad's clothes are back in style now
And his old cars kinda cool
Time takes care of the old guys
Who act like such a fool.

Every parent goes thru this
Or that's the way it seems
So I'll hope that I can keep my mind
When my kid goes thru his teens.

Dave Hungate
February 1999

Reality

Those who think there is no God
Need walk few miles the path we've trod.
To understand how each event,
Can't be a quirk or accident.

Given a choice, we wouldn't go through
The things he guides us to do.
It's all a part of his great plan
Too complicated for simple man.

Dave Hungate
February 1999

Rode Hard

Just look at some people and you can bet,
They've been rode hard and put away wet.
Try to imagine how they must have felt
When the cards of life were dealt.

They had plans, there is no doubt,
When their young lives started out.
Did take a wrong turn, did their engine explode,
Or are there too many rough spots in the road.

Some have turned sour and dread each day,
Others still happy, take time to play.
The sad carry burdens too heavy to bear,
The happy have friends and lessons to share.

Generations to come will experience the same,
When it's their turn to bat in life's game.
All we can do is tell them each fact,
Only they can decide how to react.

Dave Hungate
March 1999

Reunion

I'm going to a reunion with some dear old friends of mine,
Friendships that have lasted throughout the test of time.
Some of them for fifty years, some not quite that long,
Each person somewhat different, who helps us all be strong.

Don't talk to them of status most of them don't care,
Talk about a lifetime your joy and pain they share.
Remember those that could not come and those who passed away,
But have no dreary epilogue or tears to cloud the day.

They are still right here with us although they are imparted
Remember it was because of them that all of this got started.
The town of Green Rock is still there, but the name no longer stands.
Memories still bond us as tight as iron bands.

Few years will pass till the world forgets,
The town and where it stood,
But we'll remember always
The Green Rock brotherhood.

Dave Hungate
March 1999

Beehive

We are tiny little bees in the world's beehive.
Searching with diligence for a way to survive.
Sentenced by ourselves, to life as a slave.
Mistreated and mistrusted from womb to grave.

Serving masters that are seldom if ever seen;
Every bit as real as a king or a queen.
Chained and imprisoned, body and mind.
Unwilling or unable, escape to find.

By innocently keeping up with the rest.
Actually betraying the ones loved best.
Planning and striving for a great tomorrow.
Today has escaped us compounding our sorrow.

Most of our dreams have gone away.
Yet we continue to slave each day.
As our life slides by, we continue to lose.
Surviving each day with solitude and booze.

We did not escape but to the contrary.
We committed ourselves to solitary.
Our only goal now, we used to dread.
We plan for the day, we wake up dead.

Dave Hungate
October 1999

91

First Job

I guess I'm not sure, what was my first job.
I spent lots of years as a poor working slob.
I carried a paper when I was a kid,
But a dog on a leash made more than I did.

I worked for a while in a grocery store
Stacking shelves from ceiling to floor.
Then I got a call to set bowling pins;
If you like a bruised face and battered shins.

All we get paid was 10 cents a lane.
This wasn't a job; it's completely insane.
If you worked real hard and had good luck,
And business was steady; you might make a buck.

The best night ever was a dollar and a half.
This crappie job was just a laugh.
Then I got on at Rock Island Rail Road;
A darn good job for a kid with a load.

They paid me a Dollar Eighty- Four.
Much like a fortune to a kid that was poor.
I thought I was tough and had made the rounds.
I was just Seventeen, weighed ninety- four pounds.

I was not smart but I was no fool.
I took the job but finished High School.
It wasn't easy, you get the drift,
School all day and work second shift.

I guess that would be my first real job.
That got me started as a working slob.

Dave Hungate
April 1999

Friendships

Friends like you are Gods special gift.
Just seeing you cause spirits to lift.
A mischievous look in a passing glance.
Was that planned or happened by chance?

It doesn't matter, I knew by the look.
You were reading me like an open book.
Stories of us should be printed in Gold.
Stories that probably shouldn't be told.

Stories of families, spouses and kids.
Stories sometimes of life on the skids.
Burdens lightened by things we shared.
Knowing forever, that someone cared.

Sticking together thru ups and downs.
Acting often like ridiculous clowns.
Laughing of hot tubs and wild weekends.
Sharing in laughter that never ends.

Friends like that are so very few.
Friends that love you for being you.
Thank you for sharing my special night.
Again you have made everything right.

Dave Hungate
November 1999

Ugly or Pretty

Who decides what is pretty or ugly.
Like thinking a bear should be cuddly.
Animals, fish and birds we acquire.
Reptiles and insects not many desire.

Nature's finest art displayed on a snake.
Just thinking of makes us quiver or shake.
To degrade someone we call them a worm,
The nicest of creatures, facts confirm.

Being called a worm with bad intent,
To many, that would be a complement.
Most people wouldn't stop to pet a hog,
But love to the death the rottenest dog.

Designs on a spider are an artist's dream.
Not appreciated much so it would seem.
The same things seen it a different light
Like the moon that blesses every night.

A beautiful lover's or harvest moon.
Inspire words for singers to croon.
The very same moon in the same sky
Haunted by shadows cause us to cry.

Beauty in the eye of any beholder
Can make their heart younger or older.
Expand your mind and try not to quake.
The next time you see a beautiful snake.

Try not to act like you're walking eggs;
The worst of snakes walk on two legs.

Dave Hungate
October 1999

Writer's Group

Meeting once a Month, a writers group,
Giving each other the latest scoop.
Spirited people but gentle of mind,
No longer facing the daily grind.

Bodies and attitudes season with age.
Reading life's book, page by page.
Living more each day than some in a year,
With nothing to prove, nothing to fear.

Each one gaining the sum of the whole,
Many are accomplishing a life long goal.
Thank you so much, my writer friends,
Now let the amazing stories begin.

Stories of fact, stories of fiction.
Stories of calm, stories of action.
Thrill me again, with favorites of mine.
The stories with a loaded last line.

Dave Hungate
October 1999

Enduring Life

Why do we drink, why do we swear?
Why do we pray, why do we care?
We spend our lives like a spinning wheel,
Afraid to act, afraid to feel.

Wasting this life in which we live,
Afraid to take, afraid to give.
Weary of hurting and being hurt,
Afraid to love, and afraid to flirt.

We try to cling to something secure
A family, a job, or life that's pure.
The only sure thing, is that nothing is for sure.
Instead of living, we just endure.

Never too happy, never too sad,
Never to good, never too bad.
Is there a God, does He exist?
Others accept it, must I persist?

In finding answers that don't exist
Must we get old, before we get smart.
Must we lose our mind, must we lose our heart.

Dave Hungate
March 1999

Flight

I had some real good rides on a plane,
But I've also had some that were insane.
We headed for San Juan, Puerto Rico,
But they had problems we didn't know

We landed in Miami , Florida instead;
They unloaded passengers and went on ahead
We waited for hours and had to stay there
They wouldn't let us go anywhere.

Then finally they decided we could fly out,
But we still don't know what this was about.
Then over the speaker a new voice came
As soon as we all boarded the plane.

This is Rocky Martin your captain and guide
Welcome folks let's go for a ride.
He revved up the engines and away we went
Some of the seats even bent.

Our faces slid back and covered our ears;
There were lots of screams and even a few tears.
Rocky had flying down to an art.
We soon found out that was the easy part.

Every so often we would drop a few feet
Some got ready their maker to meet.
But luck stayed with us , San Juan was near.
We drank free drinks to cover our fear.

Then all of a sudden we came to stop.
I thought of how soon would we have to drop.
The nose of that plane went into a dive
I knew there was no way we could make it alive.

I was sure we had passed a point of no return;
Then Rocky pulled back as the engines churned.
Our faces slid down to visit our chin,
And people began to scream again.

We hit the ground like a dirty wet mop
Reversed the engines and slid to a stop.
While I still fly with relative ease
But never again with Rocky, please.

Dave Hungate
February 1999

Bleach

There was an old man who loved to bleach,
And knew it was something he had to teach.
To his friends, his children and his wife,
If he wanted them to have a good life.

He scrubbed the ceiling, walls and floor,
When that was done, he looked for more.
Counter tops, dishes and windowpane,
He drove his family nearly insane.

He scrubbed the kids with bleach every day,
'Til most of their features faded away.
He didn't do this just to be mean,
But he wanted them all cleaner than clean.

Time has passed and the children are grown,
It's time for them to be on their own.
He only had one thing more to give,
To young adults with lives to live.

To have and to hold for ever more,
So off he went to the grocery store.
When he returned, he had one for each,
Their own, very own bottle of bleach.

Dave Hungate
March 1999

Books

Books could fill on what we don't know.
We each have to learn this blow by blow.
Foolish facts, incredibly strange,
Some things never, ever change.

Some gain power because of birth right;
Others worthier fight their fight.
Living cocoons who were born in a tomb,
Destiny set while still in the womb.

With wasted lives directed by fate,
Pompous fools masquerading as great.
Ruling the world for you and me
Que sera sera, what will be will be.

I try to be positive but I'm getting warn out.
And beginning to wonder what life is about.
So many are sick, so many are broke,
This isn't life, it's just a sick joke.

The bad donate money and aspire being good,
It wouldn't be needed if they dealt as they should.
The religious say smile, this is a test,
Don't they understand we're doing our best.

I'm still so bewildered and feeling so punk.
If this is a test, I'm going to flunk.
Que sera sera—what will be will be.

Dave Hungate
March 1999

Criticism

I never met a person I didn't like,
But some are borderline.
I know there's flaws in all of them,
And I guess I've got mine.

Others have many, many faults
Which makes them easy to see.
But since I'm always looking at them
They are harder to find in me.

Before we criticize others,
I think it's time we begin,
To take a close look at ourselves
And maybe to look within.

None of my friends are perfect
And I certainly am not a saint.
But we like each other anyway,
So I'm satisfied with the ones that ain't!

Dave Hungate
March 1999

Mr. Cigarette

Mr. Cigarette is my faithful friend.
Though he may kill me in the end.
We've been together for many years.
Shared life's toil, joys and tears.

I won't smoke while in your house,
Nor would I bring a cat or mouse.
All that's needed is use your head,
To follow all rules is living dead.

Who cares if I die sometime or now,
We all have to go sometime, somehow.
All that I ask is he makes it quick.
Can't stand the thought of bein' sick.

In the meantime, I'll be moving on.
Smokin' and jokin' till I'm gone.

Dave Hungate
May 1999

Bored

How could anyone ever be bored?
With a world out there to be explored.
Each day when the sun comes up again
A brand-new day is about to begin.

A few more hours and it will be noon,
An exciting day will be over soon.
Now it is time to get some rest,
Knowing deep down we did our best.

A few more hours the sun will be up,
So we start again to fill life's cup.
Nothings as amazing as life to a child,
Amusing, confusing, meek and mild.

Each day to them is another adventure;
Just one more door for them to enter.
Maybe adults should learn from them,
And explore each day their every whim.

The longer we live the more we know.
The world every day puts on a new show.
So get up and get out, get moving on,
All too soon your life will be gone.

Dave Hungate
October 1999

Briar Bluff

Some people think we're acting a fool
When we tell of Briar Bluff school.
But I swear, I swear, we tell the truth
About the teacher who loved Babe Ruth.

Half went in the morning, half in afternoon
Because Briar Bluff just had one room.
We went to school but half a day
Most of that was spent in play.

Mr. Harris had missed his call,
His one true love was old baseball.
Things he taught aren't in a book,
Like how to dodge a sharp left hook.

How to fall, where to stand
Out of reach for his backhand.
He was mean and he was quick
And followed thru with a kick.

Some still question Mr. Harris's worth
The poorest teacher on God's earth.
These stories are true and fun to tell
Mr. Harris is dead, may he rot in hell.

Dave Hungate
February 1999

Car Accidents

These are hard cold facts I quote,
If you're listening, please take note.
Dispelling our misguided fears
Of the past one hundred years.

More have died in cars confined,
Than in all the wars combined.
Add to that just one more terror,
Ninety percent was human error.

Now as you and family ride
Along with self indulgent pride,
Please take heed and take action,
Improve this record by a fraction.

Your families' life has little effect,
No records or charts would redirect,
Your families' future depends on you
Be careful and think of what you do.

Dave Hungate
February 1999

Driving Machines

I love to look at vintage cars
Some as majestic as the stars.
I bought and sold them for many years
To drive down the street and listen to cheers.

A '57' Chevy was one of my best
I drove it to death and put it to rest.
Like playing cards and holding trump
Some of these cars make my heart thump.

I know that it's foolish to feel this way
The best cars built are built today.
Some will argue about cars of old
You'd swear that some were plated in gold.

Some of these cars were not that good
But we forget about that as I guess we should.
Some of them literally fell apart
When it got cold, few would start.

But I love these cars just the same
And it's a healthy hearty enjoyable game.
So what if they didn't have quality or safety built in
Just look at their beautiful, beautiful skin.

They each had character so fondness has grown
They are a pleasure to drive and fun to own.
So enjoy the cars that you own and drive
It seems, as some are almost alive.

Your car is just a car for now,
But the day will come when you wonder how.
You could have driven a car that was so great,
But you didn't enjoy it until too late.

It will bring you pride and maybe sorrow
If your car become a classic tomorrow.

Dave Hungate
February 1999

Grandson

I think God had a contest
And I'm the one who won.
Because the grandest prize of all
Was the world's best grandson.

The world is full of fine young men,
But Zach is not the same.
Since he is the greatest,
He needs the greatest name.

At school, at home, or anywhere at all,
He's the best at everything, including playing ball.
He will have a lot more names
Before his life is through.

Champion, leader and genius, just to name a few,
Or maybe he'll be lucky and receive a call,
To be somebody's papa,
The grandest name of all.

Dave Hungate (Papa)
February 1999

Gulf Coast

While traveling around America's gulf coast,
And trying to decide where we liked the most.
Biloxi was first so we thought it was the best,
But that was before we visited all the rest.

Staying a few nights on Alabama's gulf shore,
We knew that for certain we just had to see more.
The next on our list was Pensacola Beach,
It was not very far and within our reach.

We unloaded the car and got settled in,
And knew it was time for the fun to begin.
We went next door to the Bay Side Grill,
Where the food was so good it gave us a thrill.

After lunch we walked a beach of white sand.
The weather was great and the view was grand.
Waves rose like mountains from out of nowhere
As warm ocean breezes flowed through your hair.

White capped waves that rose to a height
Making you happy you're not a sailor tonight.
Beaches, great beaches everywhere you go,
That gives the impression of new fallen snow.

There is no such thing as finding the best,
Each one keeps trying to outdo the rest.
Mother Nature never rests or takes any slack,
One thing is for certain that we will be back.

Dave Hungate
March 2000

Island Vacation

As you head on a beautiful island vacation,
Let's put a little twist on the situation.
What must the people who live there think,
About the people who come here to drink?

They have everything but cause a fuss,
About coming to live in poverty with us.
Maybe having money affects their brain,
What attraction could an island contain?

They get sand and pebbles in their shoes,
And sunburn easy whenever they snooze.
What lesson on clothing did they miss?
Who in the world would dress like this?

Is this some kind of a sad sadistic joke,
As they leave hung-over, sunburned and broke?
This wouldn't be so bad, but somehow I fear
Given a choice, they'll come back next year.

Dave Hungate
February 2000

Laws

Why do we have ridiculous laws?
And how much grief must they cause?
They persecute people like you and me
Then turn the thieves and murderers free.

It's our own fault and that a fact
We just complain and fail to act.
We live in a country that gives us a voice
But we do nothing—that's our choice.

We should stand up and cause a fuss
But it doesn't directly involve us.
So we just stand back and swallow our pride,
And let the wrong people go for a ride.

I include myself when I speak with disgust,
Of how we set back and violate trust.
Rape and murder will be okay
As long as you have the money to pay.

Or maybe we'll make a ridiculous claim
Let the poor guy go, because he's insane.
If they're really insane, we should take care of them
But never, ever let them out again.

And once again we'll just complain
And once again we'll all refrain
From getting involved or causing a fuss
After all it didn't involve us.

So we'll continue living each day
And continue looking the other way.
Our standards will continue to be double
Until we ourselves get in trouble.

Dave Hungate
February 1999

Memories

I've read poems that were strange
From poets who cover a wide range
But none can chill me to the bone
Like things I think of on my own.

When I think of yesteryear
Joy and sadness brings a tear.
Have I finally lost my mind?
Or do I need this to unwind.

Haunting memories good and bad
Of things we've seen and fun we've had.
Alone at midnight calm and still
Reflecting sometimes brings a chill.

Come morning we will meet the day
And go about our usual way.
To live our lives so hard and fast
Repeating mistakes of the past.

Inflicting wounds that cannot heal
And judge ourselves with no appeal.
Most scars in life are self-inflicted
That could be avoided and predicted.

Ghosts that hide within us all
Waiting to haunt at beckoned call.
Strange books that fill our library shelves
But none are stranger than ourselves.

Dave Hungate
February 1999

Neighbor

To help your neighbor without a fee
Is to help yourself much more than he.
You may be tired, but have peace of mind,
Which brings comfort, hard to find.

All he got was his work done
But you feel good and had fun.
It builds self- esteem and gives you pride
Which creates self worth deep inside.

Dave Hungate
February 1999

Ole What's his Name

How soon we forget when people retire
Or worse yet the ones who expire.
No sense getting mad, we're all the same
Trying to remember "ole what's his name."

We worked with him for many years
And shared with him a couple of beers.
You remember, he was short and fat
And always wore a silly hat.

We remember where he lived and what he drove
His kids went to school at Walnut Grove.
Our mind goes blank and it's a shame
But can't quite remember, what's his name.

Dave Hungate
February 1999

Pastor Appreciation

The order of the day which was received
Is bigger than anyone ever conceived.
A thank you for pastor appreciation,
And thirty plus years of dedication.

Sharing in happiness as some were married
Sharing in sadness as some were buried.
There are no re-paying things like that,
Nothing that's worthy of Bob and Pat.

Nelson's and we, with lives entwined
Share more than most congregations combined.
Thank you so much for the things you do,
Especially Pat, she's got Bob too.

Dave Hungate
October 1999

Retirement

We spent our lives trying to make a buck
And did pretty well with hard work and luck.
It seemed for years, there was never enough
And sometimes things got mighty rough.

It didn't seem to matter how much we made
It was all gone when the bills were paid.
We spent too much according to some
Traveling with the kids and having fun.

But the memories are priceless to us now
And we always managed to get by somehow.
If you earned a little more than the bills would take
Sure as the devil, something would break.

Appliances, cars or just a flat tire,
Somehow something would go haywire.
The kids are grown so we're going to spend
What little is left before life ends.

We'd like to leave the kids a bunch
But it'll be gone, or that's our hunch.
If we don't spend what's in the nest
Doctors or rest homes will get the rest.

So we're going out in a blaze of fire
That's our plan as we retire.

Dave Hungate
February 1999

Sad, Sad Eyes

We met a beautiful girl with sad, sad eyes.
Which led us to question the how and whys.
I spoke to her and she gave me a smile,
Her heart is okay at least for a while.

You can tell with smile if a light goes on.
They may be lost buy not totally gone.
She seemed so young, in her 30's I guess.
Her eyes told a story of like in a mess.

She is young enough to start again.
We hope she does, we want her to win.

Dave Hungate
June 1999

Tax Time

Tax time again, I can hardly wait
But Uncle Sam says don't be late.
I start out good most every year
But approach tax time with greatest fear.

Nothing can make my mind go blank
Like thoughts of G. Men, pulling rank.
I know there are records I must keep
Before I allow myself to sleep.

Each year I keep records I know I should
For a month or two I do real good.
Slowly I begin again to fall back
And fail to keep my records on track.

I lie to myself and calmly say
Tax time is almost a year away.
Then it's time to file and I pay too much tax
Which is my own fault for being so lax.

When, oh, when will I ever learn?
To keep the money I work to earn.
This year I must do it right
I must try with all might.

How many times have I said the same?
But they make the rules; I must play the game.
I must try and try and try and try
To get it right before I die.

When my body has no more life
They'll take some from my children or wife.
To win this game is my solemn goal
Before they decide to tax my soul.

Dave Hungate
February 1999

Tough Kids

I can relate to kids in trouble
I was small and poor, so I got double.
I wasn't brave and I sure wasn't tough.
But I learned as a kid when enough was enough.

Everybody thought they could push me around
But all I could do was stand my ground.
I always got whipped, had my face in the dirt,
But I tried to make sure the other guy got hurt.

They found out that if they knocked on my door
I'd answer their call ready for more.
I try real hard to respect authority
But I'll treat them like they treat me.

Like an old sailor said.
"I'll walk the plank,
But I'll take no nonsense from any rank.

It's a wonder my life turned out so good
I didn't always do the things that I should.
When I see a tough kid, I see an uncut gem,
But how in the world could I ever reach him.

Teenage years are the roughest of all
And we don't dare just let them fall.
They'll be our leaders very soon
Some of them will go to the moon.

We must save them no matter the cost
Cause if we lose the, we all have lost.

Dave Hungate
March 1999

Veterans

I know in my heart that I have no right
But sometimes I sit alone at night
And think of the veterans who came home
Only to find themselves alone.

We seem to give honor to the dead
But forget the ones who only bled.
They lost their feet, legs and arms,
Most certainly lost their childish charms.

They gave their soul some gave their mind,
And returned home only to find
They had fought the fight but lost the race,
Life at home had kept its' pace.

As they fought an awful war
Sometimes wondering why—what for?
The ones at home had gone to school
Now they stood out like an ignorant fool.

Companies hire the educated
And promote the graduated.
Once again it's the veterans loss,
The old draft dodger is now their boss.

How many times must they give?
And how many hells must they live?
How much longer can we afford
Not to give their just reward?

Dave Hungate
February 1999

120

Who Is This God?

Who is this God they talk about?
Some are calm while other must shout.
To tell of this God with incredible wit
They love everyone and will kill to prove it.

They'll even bomb children and widows for good
Some would destroy the world if they could.
They give their life and use their last breath
Trying to secure a place after death.

The world's best scholars cannot understand
A subject so vast, confusing or grand.
I choose to live this life instead
And let my creator take care of the dead.

Even the very worst skeptic by far
Need only to look at a tree or a star.
An ocean, a mountain, a child at birth
Or just a simple look at the earth.

Each square foot holds mysteries untold
Of life, plants and minerals or gold.
It is smart and good to love each other
And treat everyone as you would a brother.

I think the Master is doing just fine
And He did all this with no help of mine.

Dave Hungate
February 1999

Working Forever

I guess I'll be working the last day I live.
My boat still floats, but leaks like a sieve.
We talk cost of living and what it may take,
It always ends up a little more than I make.

If I get a raise or have a great windfall,
Something will happen that takes it all.
They say it's my fault for not planning ahead.
If I spent any less I might as well be dead.

I wanted some fun while young and alive,
I've never had desires to just survive.
Some shirk duties as Fathers and Mothers,
By trying too hard to keep up with others.

My family and I have little to regret.
The travels we shared we'll never forget.
Maybe I did do a few things wrong,
But who ever thought I'd live this long.

We all must remember to enjoy today,
You can't take it with you anyway.

Dave Hungate
February 2000

Life

Life would be funny if it wasn't so sad,
It's nice to be good, but more fun to be bad.
We work all our lives for a few years of rest,
And find that we liked past years the best.

We work all year to get a few weeks off,
To travel and swim or fish or golf.
Go camping or biking or live like a bum,
Not good for all, but great for some.

If forced to do things we like so well,
It would make our lives a living hell.
So enjoy, enjoy, enjoy each day,
Stop and smell those roses along the way.

We are too soon old and too late smart,
And hide the important things in our heart.
It's hard to accept but it's a known fact,
No matter how good we put on an act.

We don't get better we just get old,
And few have good health or treasures of gold.
So life has a lesson for you and for me,
It's true the best things in life are free.

The sooner we learn and start to enjoy,
The long we have to enjoy,
Enjoy!
Enjoy!

Dave Hungate
March 1999

Waterfront

He's a fixture on the waterfront a kind old gentle man.
He just goes on from day-to-day helping where he can.
Some may think him beggar or at least that he is broke.
That's the way he wants it; that's his private joke.

He gives and gives and gives but never does he take.
Never do the people know he give more than they make.
Nor do they know it was him who took the time to pray.
He walks a different path in life, a disciple in his way.

His prayers are all for others or guidance in his deeds.
He's thanking God for blessings by filling others needs.
There may be no water in the waterfront he walks
And you may not know you met him just by how he talks.

His words are sometimes vulgar; he smokes or has a drink.
He doesn't have all answers nor care what people think.
He sometimes gives a handout or listens to them sob.
But doesn't listen much to that, he'll help them find a job.

There are people just like him, to church they will not go.
Afraid of being hypocrites, who are putting on a show.
Some of them would like to go, for them it would be fun.
How could they feel unwelcome "My God" what have we done?

This little man in question lives deep within us all.
Reach out a hand and help someone, He's waiting for your call.

Dave Hungate
May 1999

Knowledge

Is our soul in our heart or in our head?
Does our soul keep living when we are dead?
What's the difference in a mind or a brain?
How many mysteries does our body contain?

Is there any such as a spirit or ghost?
Why are they what people fear most?
Think of sixth sense , seventh or eighth.
Control of them would sure be great.

What about answers that come in the night?
Knowing by a feeling when something's right.
Is there any such thing as being possessed?
Is that an excuse for sin not confessed?

What makes us serious or act like a clown?
What changes our attitude up or down?
Everything in the world has a purpose.
All our knowledge hasn't scratched the surface.

Dave Hungate
December 1999

Computer

I bought a new computer, it was pink.
It was so good, I swear it could think.
We traveled everywhere on the web and the net,
It was a better companion than any woman I've met.

It did everything I wanted to do
It was my dream, so I named it Sue.
She worked real hard and stayed on track
Never got grouchy, never talked back.

She was beautiful and had mystic powers.
I loved her so much I brought her flowers.
She was as good as good could be
She proved over and over how she loved me.

Then all of a sudden her screen began to flutter
It soon got worse, she began to spit and sputter.
I called a repairman, who had good sense,
I said please fix her, spare no expense.

To my amaze, he found my great computer
Had found herself an electronic suitor.
Well I fixed her; I fixed that witch,
I unplugged her and gave her a pitch.

I never even look at computers anymore
Who knows what life has in store?
But if I ever look again for a lovely pearl
Please let it be a real live girl!

Dave Hungate
February 1999

David, My Son

For so many, many years I did not have a son.
Then the Lord saw fit to finally send me one.
I love my daughters dearly, but needed a son too
To fill a special void, that only a son can do.

Maybe the years of waiting, was some sort of test,
So when a son came to me, he could be the best.
This Son that I was getting would also bear my name.
I wouldn't want to harm him or ever bring him shame.

I try to be about as fair as any man can be,
Judging all sons fairly, the best belongs to me.
Even the Son of a Son of a gun,
Gives purpose to life and can be such fun.

I thank the lord each day for that perfect gift,
Although no thanks are worthy of a gift like this.

David Hungate

ABOUT THE AUTHOR

Dave Hungate, a retired supervisor, has been writing poems most of his adult life. His writings, in general, are about every day happenings. He has combined his wit and perspective about ordinary people and events that have or may touch the lives of many. He started the book as a dare from a coworker and hopes to continue pursuing his dream of writing and publishing his poetry.